# NOTHING **TO SHOW** FOR IT

## THE STUDENT ATHLETE'S RULE BOOK FOR SUCCESS

VERNON JACKSON ESQ

Nothing To Show For It
Copyright © 2014 Vernon Jackson

ISBN-10: 0692355251
ISBN-13: 978-0-692-35525-1

Publishing Consultant Rebecca Cerria Montgomery/RM Consultants
Cover and layout design by Steven Plummer/SPDesign

# TABLE OF CONTENTS

L ET'S GET STRAIGHT to the point. You having athletic talent and being offered an athletic scholarship does not guarantee you a damn thing in life. If you are not prepared for the traps that lie ahead for you, you will waste everything that you worked for and end up with ABSOLUTELY NOTHING TO SHOW FOR IT. You do not want to be that 40 year old guy hanging on the same block that he grew up on bragging about how many touchdowns he scored in high school because that is pretty much all he ever accomplished in life. This book will give you the straightforward rules on how to utilize your talent to improve your life instead of wasting it.

The knowledge that went into the development of these rules came from my life experiences, observations and research. I was raised in poverty almost entirely by my mom. I was able to overcome many obstacles and earn a scholarship to the University of Iowa. I played there for two years until knee injuries ended my career. Thereafter I finished my degree, graduated from law school and began my career as a criminal defense attorney. I will speak more in depth about my life later in the book, but the actual rules given are what you should focus on. Follow these rules and your chances of success skyrocket. Ignore them and your chances of becoming another failure statistic skyrocket.

## Who I'm Talking To:

This book has a narrow focus, but a universal application. I wrote this book specifically to warn the young, black, urban male who has overcome all obstacles and earned the opportunity to gain a paid for college education by utilizing his academic and athletic ability. I target this group because: (1) The opportunity that they are faced with is probably for them a once in a life time do or die opportunity and they literally can't afford to waste it. (2) If they are not careful they can so very easily blow this opportunity and end up back in the inner city without an education and any certain path toward success. Because of a lack of forewarning, an improper mindset and many schools failing to provide guidelines like the ones in this book, a large number of the young black males that I speak of invest their energy, bodies, sweat and blood creating billions in profits for their universities, and yet end up a few years later with absolutely NOTHING TO SHOW FOR IT. This common trend is a despicable shame. Too many of these talented young men fall into one of the traps that I list next, and end up back in their old neighborhoods with nothing to show for their efforts besides damaged bones, joints and ligaments, and old stories about their past gridiron greatness.

While this book does have a targeted audience in mind, the warnings it provides will aid all potential college student athletes, regardless of race, class or family background. Anyone given the opportunity to play college sports and receive a paid-for education should be thrilled, but also aware of the risks and temptations that await them. Any student athlete can fall into the traps that I will outline below, and so reading this book would provide beneficial warnings to all.

I will use examples of both college and professional football players, many of which I know personally or have extensive knowledge about. Because football is what I am most experienced in, mainly football players will be discussed, though all high school and college athletes face similar pitfalls. I will be as concise as possible, as this book should be used as a guide for both the athletes and their parents.

# MY PURPOSE IN WRITING THIS BOOK:

THIS BOOK IS a list of warnings and guidelines. The aim of these tenets is to keep young black males from being pawns to the University's money-machine, while receiving none of the tools needed to have a quality life after college. College athletics is a billion dollar industry made rich by its workers, the student athletes. Therefore it is sad and shameful for so many of them to end up with absolutely nothing to show for their efforts.

Many of the most talented young football players in America come from black inner cities. So many of them grew up in challenging circumstances where poverty, crime and the lack of a father made football seem to be the only possible way out. Ray Lewis of the Baltimore Ravens, Justin Houston of the Kansas City Chiefs, Patrick Willis of the San Francisco Forty Niners and Dez Bryant of the Dallas Cowboys, are just a few examples of this trend. The list goes on and on. Because of the circumstances these young men were raised in and the vast differences between their environments at home and the environments they are thrown into on large college campuses, there are heightened risks that they will fall into certain devastating traps.

Below are the most common pit falls that young black athletes fall into. Each of these traps can cause a high level prep athlete to end up after 3 or 4 years of endless work, training, and sacrifice, with absolutely nothing to show for it.

# HAVING NO IDENTITY OR PURPOSE IN LIFE ASIDE FROM FOOTBALL:

A VERY LARGE NUMBER of young black men are taught early on in life that football, and sports in general, are not only fun and rewarding, but also their only way out of the ghetto. Parents, relatives and teachers may not intentionally teach these boys this lesson but the lesson is none the less thoroughly taught through their actions. Often parents put footballs into their kids' hands way before they've handed them their first book. These parents show up and cheer hard at football games but fail to even go to parent teacher conferences to discuss their kid's grades. These young men receive a great deal of respect and admiration in their communities because of their football abilities. Sadly, the academic prowess and progress of these young men doesn't receive nearly the same level of attention and admiration. Even teachers praise and admire these young men for their exploits on the field, while turning a blind eye to their inability to read at grade level. On top of all of this, many of the females on campus pursue, date and mingle with these young men solely because they are athletes. As a result football often becomes the main (and sometimes only) source of self-esteem and positive gratification in the lives of these young men.

I speak from personal experience (and observation of many young athletes) when I say that growing up in this way can be devastating. These athletes begin to link their self-worth with their on the field performance, and so performing well on the field takes on a level of importance that it never should have. Life is good when they are performing well, but when they are not serious problems can occur.

Personally, when I would arrive at a family function as a teenager, the conversation would immediately switch to football. What kind of workouts I was doing, what college did I want to play football at and how my high school team would perform that season; were always hot topics. Football occupied the majority of my time, thoughts and energy. It is a very dangerous thing for a person to base his whole self-image, self-worth and all of his life aspirations on a sport that could forever be taken away with one injury.

A well adjusted, balanced young black male growing up under these circumstances must have a strong spiritual base, an understanding of the importance of education, and an awareness that one day he will have to live without football. These young men must know who they are, what their purpose in life is and that one day the applause and cameras will be gone. One day they will have to function and provide for themselves and their families, without tackling or throwing touchdowns. A parent must not put an over-emphasis on their kid's athletic endeavors while neglecting all of the child's other endeavors. Parents, as well as coaches, must not allow these young men to become so absorbed in the game of football that they have no identity or life goals apart from the sport. Parents and coaches who fail to force these young men to consider life beyond the gridiron, do them a grave disservice and set them up for serious internal strife in the future.

When I made the tough, but smart decision not to continue to risk my health by pushing forward with my football career in the face of chronic knee problems, I was finally forced to sit down and consider just who I would be aside from being a defensive tackle. Since the age of 9, football had largely defined who I was as a person but for the first time that was about to change. I had to ask myself: (1) What besides football makes me valuable as a person? (2) What in life will I be passionate about aside from sacking QBs? and; (3) What will I talk to my family and friends about now?

Years after I hung up the cleats people back home would continue to ask how football was going and when I was going to turn pro. They could not separate Vernon Jackson (the person) from Vernon Jackson (the defensive tackle). In addition they were unable to understand that there are many other things a black man can be successful at in life beyond just football. In many ways these people took my leaving football harder than I did. Because my mom had given me a strong spiritual grounding I was able to let go of the sport that had occupied most my entire life and know there was still plenty to be grateful for and enthusiastic about. I was able to put the same effort into my academics, which lead to me becoming an honor student and a leader on my campus. I grew into a leader in many different spheres on campus, from the Black Student Union to Student Government and the 2008 Iowa campaign for then presidential candidate Barack Obama. Sadly, many athletes are unable to make such a transition.

Many young black males currently competing in high school and college sports are completely unprepared to face life in the absence of their beloved sport. I have seen players continue to try and hang on to their football careers, disregarding medical evidence which clearly showed that such a decision would likely be devastating to their health. I have seen players who finish their college careers and are unable to get drafted or signed by an NFL team, who instead of moving into the next phase of their lives, seek to continue playing football in any capacity possible (whether it be arena football, semi-pro football, flag football etc). Some of these young men do this simply out of love for the game, but many do it because they cannot separate their identities as individuals from their identities as athletes.

As a young athlete you must have life goals that are important to you beyond the playing field. You must be able to separate yourself as an individual from yourself as a full back or strong safety. There must be other things that you are enthusiastic about. Think about these things now and do not limit your outlook on life to catching and tackling.

# VIEWING COLLEGE AS SIMPLY "PREP FOR THE PROS"

EVERY YOUNG BLACK male who is able to overcome an impoverished, challenging background and make it to college must step on campus from day one with an understanding that his main goal is to get a meaningful degree; and that this will benefit him for the rest of his life. True, some athletes will go pro and have long professional careers, after which money will never be an issue for them; however THIS IS NOT THE CASE FOR THE VAST MAJORITY OF COLLEGE ATHLETES. On the average, an NFL player's career lasts only 3 to 4 years. That is it. After that the former athlete will still have the responsibility of providing for himself and his family. Statistics demonstrate that black men have greater difficulty competing in the job market than white men and without a degree the task is made even harder. These facts make the stakes much higher for these student athletes.

When I arrived at the University of Iowa I thought the coaching staff there was going to prepare me for a long NFL career, that was the mindset of many of my teammates and is the mindset of most highly recruited athletes. This belief can lead to the academic aspect of college being pushed to the back burner (if it is on the stove at all). I've seen athletes miss as many classes as they could find an excuse to miss, leisurely sleep through class just to wake up in time for practice, search Facebook the entire time they sat in study hall (as opposed to studying) and then act surprised when they are academically ineligible to compete. I've seen highly ranked prep athletes come into college with no understanding of the crucial importance of getting a degree, and flunk out after one year of partying hard and sleeping through class. This phenomenon is so very sad, but true.

One of the most well known examples of this phenomenon is former Miami Hurricane linebacker Willie Williams. Any coach that has ever dealt with Williams will attest to the fact that his athletic ability was extraordinary and rare. He was a true specimen on the football field. The media that chronicled his troubled life throughout high school, multiple colleges and a failed attempt to go pro, attest to the fact that he saw college (and high school as well) as simply a walk-through to the NFL. It is well documented that Williams' teen years were marred by multiple run-ins with the law. Despite this, Williams was the prototype for an NFL linebacker, and colleges knew it. Williams was awarded a scholarship to the University of Miami but shortly thereafter he transferred because he was not made an immediate starter. He ended up at Louisville for a short time, but was unable to govern his personal conduct in any reasonable manner. Again he found himself in trouble with the law and kicked off of the team. Williams landed at a much smaller institution where he continued to dominate on the field, but never grasped the fact that college was not simply training for the NFL. After bouncing around multiple colleges Williams was left with no degree and never did make it in the NFL. His trouble with the law continued even after his playing days ended and Williams has essentially nothing to show for all of his crushing tackles and QB sacks.

My freshman year at the University of Iowa I roomed with a highly recruited fullback from the state of Florida. This young man was a four star recruit and had received offers from many of the largest college football powerhouses in the nation. He was big, fast and agile. He had been raised in the urban core of a large Florida city and his family life had not been ideal. He represents precisely the type of student athlete this book is specifically aimed at. From the moment he stepped foot on campus at the University of Iowa, his priorities (as manifested by his actions) were football first, partying second, and academics last. This young man would party late into the night and sleep it off during class time the next day. He chased women on campus as if that were a sport in and of itself. My own sleep was interrupted on multiple occasions due to the late night "activities" of this young man and his female companions. He was constantly in trouble with the strength and conditioning staff because he couldn't control his weight (excess drinking has that affect). Studying was not something this young man was interested in. After one year of endless fun the young man had a GPA that was embarrassing and was ineligible to continue to compete. He left the University of Iowa without a degree, or anything else to show for his endeavor in the Midwest.

On so many occasions I would head to a morning class and my roommate would still be sleeping peacefully in his bed. I was a little envious of the leisurely lifestyle he was leading and I wondered if it was possible to go through college and succeed with such little discipline and academic effort. My questions were quickly answered when grades were released and this partying fullback was no longer on campus. It is my hope that young black student athletes will read this book and realize that college is not simply a 3 or 4-year stopping point before the pros. I hope they will realize that college offers the opportunity to expand their horizons intellectually and socially. I hope these young men will seize the academic and career opportunities, as well as the athletic opportunities that come with a college athletic scholarship. I hope they will choose the path opposite that taken by my freshman year roommate.

Many of the black athletes that make the mistake of going through 3 or 4 years of college and leaving without a degree will end up back in their old neighborhoods, struggling to make a living. There will be no cheering crowds and no big parties to attend, and the reality of competing for a job will hit them in the face. They will realize then, the importance of an education and wish they had taken advantage of the opportunity they once had. I BEG OF EVERY YOUNG BLACK MALE WHO HAS COME FROM CHALLENGING CIRCUMSTANCES AND EARNED AN ATHLETIC SCHOLARSHIP-PLEASE DON'T LEAVE THAT INSTITUTION WITHOUT A COLLEGE DEGREE. PLEASE.

# BECOMING A PRODUCT OF A FOOTBALL FACTORY

L ARGE ATHLETIC SCHOOLS rake in billions as a result of the efforts of their athletes, and there are two sad facts that must be stated in relation to that point. (1) Many large institutions function as simply "football factories" and do not truly emphasize the importance of academics to their athletes. As long as the young man has just good enough a G.P.A to be cleared to compete, the coaching staff is happy and will not push the young man to insure he actually graduates; (2) institutions of this nature will go as far as to steer a student toward a "less challenging major" than what he desired, simply to insure he does not fall behind and become ineligible to compete. I know of black college football players who were encouraged not to major in something "complicated" like engineering, and to instead major in something that would allow them more time to focus on watching film and preparing for that week's opponent. A college that takes this approach with their student athletes is a selfish, greedy institution, and the student athlete who allows this to happen becomes nothing more than a profit generating pawn that will be left with nothing to show for the work, sweat and pain he invests in the school's athletic program.

A stunning example of these athletic factory schools came to light in early 2014 when it was revealed that many of the basketball players at the University of North Carolina COULD NOT READ. Some were reading below a 5th grade level, but "somehow" they were able to remain academically elgible to compete. What in the hell is such a young man going to do to take care of himself once the game of basketball is no longer providing his every need?

Parents do not allow your child to attend a "football factory" or "basketball factory." Make sure that the coaching staff and academic support staff at the institution your child is to attend, truly care about the academic success of the student athletes. If a college coach comes to your home to recruit your son and highlights everything the athletic program has to offer (excellent coaches, great facilities, wonderful fans) but fails to mention the program's graduation rates or academic support program, this is a sign that that coach works for a football factory. If the program does not have in place measures to make sure every player is attending his classes and that every player has the tutors and academic support staff that he needs, this is further evidence that the program is just a football factory. Also, parents don't let your children (or yourselves) forget that college is first and foremost about getting an education.

# "I WANNA GO HOME SYNDROME"

ANOTHER TROUBLING TENDENCY I have noticed with many young black college football athletes is to leave the school that they initially signed with based on the fact that they do not become starters right away, have some sort of problem with a coach at the school, or experience any minor discomfort at the University. Overwhelmingly this has been a terrible idea, and has turned out poorly for the athletes that I've known. I've seen this same story line play out many times. The athlete will enthusiastically sign on at the school of his choosing and at the first sign that things are not going perfectly according to his plan, he calls home and tells his friends and family, "Hey, I'm going to transfer somewhere closer to home" as if that will magically fix the situation. It is my opinion that many athletes do this simply because they are home sick and there is no one telling them to simply grow up, be independent and stick it out. It is a fact that out of the many times that I've seen this, it results in catastrophe for the athlete 95% of the time. They often get back home to their old environments, begin running with their old circles again and soon forget about school and sports all together.

The most glaring and sad example of this that I can remember is an athlete out of Orlando, Florida, by the name of Carlton Christian. This young man grew up directly across the street from me and my family, in a rough area known as Mercy Drive. He grew up to be a 6'5 phenomenon on the hardwood and dominated at the varsity level for 3 years at Maynard Evans High School. Carlton was big, fast, an excellent shooter and explosive leaper. His ability was second to none. He earned a full scholarship to Marquette University at the very time when that program was just coming off of a run at the national title under the leadership of Dwayne Wade. The hopes of the entire city were upon Carlton's shoulders as he went off to Wisconsin, but after a year Carlton decided to "transfer somewhere closer to home." He planned to transfer to the University of Central Florida and carry on his academic and basketball careers right next to where it all began! Perfect right? Absolutely not. Within a year of being back in Orlando, Carlton had been arrested for multiple felonies, crushing his basketball dreams. To date, Carlton has not finished school and his basketball glories are nothing but memories. Just being closer to home did not magically fix anything; it did however allow Carlton to fall victim to the same negative forces he had worked so hard to escape.

I often hear of young men transferring closer to home to be near elderly or ailing loved ones. There is certainly value in making such a decision. You can never blame a kid for wanting to be close to his grandmother who raised him, if she is terminally ill. That being said, I must caution the specific athletes at whom this book is aimed to be very thoughtful and careful when making such a decision. For other athletes the choice to go back home does not mean going back to an impoverished inner city filled with crime and easy opportunities to slip into trouble, for the urban black male it does. Even going home for a valiant reason can turn out to be a huge mistake. Uprooting, trying to get settled into a new university and team environment, all while trying to look out for an ailing family member, is not easy and is not something you are obligated to do. Old friends can pull you down and I am certain that if grandma had a choice between you coming home to provide her with emotional support (and slipping back into your old environment) as opposed to you staying in school (calling her on the phone each night) but leaving with a degree, she would pick the latter.

I plead with young black athletes that come from rough areas, DO NOT THINK TRANSFERING CLOSER TO HOME IS A FIX-ALL. Your old neighborhood will always be there for you to return to, I promise the hood is going nowhere. You owe it to your neighborhood to return and build it when you are able, but it helps no one for you to leave the school you obviously considered best for you (at the first sign of hardship) simply to be closer to home. It almost never works out as planned. If there is a serious issue at the school you first chose to attend and it simply cannot be resolved, then maybe transferring is something you should consider. However, simply not being a starter right away, or not liking one of the coaches on the coaching staff, is NOT such a reason. When I got to the University of Iowa, which is over 90% white, after growing up in inner city Orlando (which is the exact opposite) I was thousands of miles from home, homesick and experiencing serious cultural shock. Despite my initial discomfort, I was not under the illusion that simply moving back closer to home was the right thing to do. I knew I needed to get a degree and finish what I'd started, so I stayed and stuck it out. From what I've seen, this is normally the best path to take.

# WOMEN JERSEY CHASERS AND STAR STRUCK ONE NIGHTERS:

THIS NEXT TOPIC is one that is very complex as it involves issues of race, class and divergent cultures. To give the warnings that I must give on this topic, political correctness must take a back seat. I speak on this issue from experience, up close observation and analysis of other well-known events in the sports world.

Many young black athletes from inner city lower class areas sign letters of intent and soon thereafter find themselves in worlds totally different (racially and culturally) than their home environments. These new conditions present these young men with wonderful opportunities to broaden their horizons, learn, expand and grow, but these new environments also present many serious risks. I speak from personal experience on this point, as I attended a high school in Orlando that was 90% black and most of the students came from families at or below the poverty line. From

Orlando I went to the University of Iowa where the student body is over 90% white and mostly from middle to upper class families. I would often be the only black male in lecture halls containing over 250 students. I had to make a few adjustments to get used to this.

At large Universities, there exist (what we called in my college days) "Jersey Chasers." A Jersey Chaser is a female who for one reason or another only wants to date athletes. For some Jersey Chasers it is the physique of an athlete, for some it is the social status that comes with dating an athlete, and for others it is the possibility that the athlete might one day go pro and make millions of dollars. This type of woman can be a destructive force in the life of a young male athlete, mainly because she does not really love or care about the young man as a person. What she loves is the position that he holds. When things go wrong in the relationship, this type of woman can be particularly bitter and hateful in how she reacts. This is so because she was never truly emotionally attached to the individual himself, but to the status of dating an athlete. These women are more prone to get the police involved in any sort of spat between the two, maybe because they know this action will also thrust them further into the spot light. Any such complaint (even if it does not lead to an arrest or conviction) permanently tarnishes the young man's reputation, distracts from his ultimate goals, and harms his future. This type of woman will leave one football player and soon be dating another.

The issue of Jersey Chasers is further complicated by race,

though a Jersey Chaser can certainly be of any race. Many young black athletes interact with a large number of white women for the first time while attending college. Many of these young white women grow up in homes where their dads are extremely passionate about the sports teams of his alma mater, and the girls learn to be just as excited. These dads often know the names of the individual players on his college team, and he often idolizes or glorifies these players. Their daughters mimic that behavior. The daughter often goes off to attend the college that dad attended and loves so much. In her mind, dating one of those glorified athletes could offer a great thrill. Often this athlete is a black male from an entirely different world than the one the girl is from (culturally, racially and economically). The danger as a result is that she doesn't truly know, understand or care about the actual person the young man is, but again, the position that he holds.

Such a relationship can be very harmful to the athlete, as well as the young woman. Many of these relationships end quickly because there is not a real foundation upon which the relationship can grow. Some of these young men will remain in such a relationship simply for the perks that come along with it. For example, normally the girl is from a higher socio-economic status so while the young man has to depend on whatever scholarship money he gets, the girl can always call home to daddy for some quick money. A Jersey Chaser is often very willing to spend money on an athlete just to keep him happy and to secure her position. At the end of the day, most of these relationships do not end well. Young black males headed off to large institutions of higher learning must be aware of this phenomenon, and be very careful about who they date and socialize with.

In addition to the Jersey Chaser, there exists on every campus where sports are important, (what I have termed) the "Star Struck One Nighter." This type of woman can also be of any race, but again race further complicates the issue. This type of woman normally has no real desire to be in a long-term relationship with the young black athlete. She may simply not want such a relationship or may choose to avoid it because she knows her family would not approve of it (this is because even today it would cause an uproar in many well-to-do white families if the daughter were to bring home a black guy). Regardless, the Star Struck One Nighter is driven by her curiosity about the sexual prowess of these young black stars. More often than not the Star Struck One Nighter has heard rumors from friends and popular culture about the sexual ability of these young men. This type of girl normally just wants a one-night experience, or casual sexual encounters with the young man. In addition, she often meets athletes at parties or bars where alcohol and or drugs are clouding the judgment of both parties (more on drugs and alcohol later). This type of woman is anxious to "see what all the hype is about," and all too often the athlete does not have the will power and discipline to turn her down. I WARN YOU YOUNG BLACK ATHLETES NOW, YOU MUST TURN HER DOWN.

The list of terrible consequences that can flow from these casual one night sexual encounters is endless. I will mention a few of the main ones. Number one: STDs- two careless, intoxicated, immature individuals driven by sexual desire often forget about protection, in addition to the fact that there are some diseases even condoms won't always protect against. I have seen young male athletes contract STDs from one passionate sexual encounter with a star struck female only to forever suffer the consequences. I've seen athletes have to miss games because of "injuries" that they sustained while competing with a Star Struck One Nighter. One very serious example of this involved a close friend of mine at the University of Iowa. He met a Star Struck One Nighter and simply made out with her. As a result he contracted the "kissing disease" Mononucleosis or "Mono." My friend was a defensive back from Wisconsin and had fought hard to earn a spot on the roster. As a result of his disease though, he missed many classes as well as practices and weight-room sessions. His grades dropped and he was cut from the team. This was certainly a harsh price to pay for trying to make it to second base with a girl he'd just met, but I've seen far worse.

Maybe the most devastating consequence that I have seen result from a young black athlete entertaining a Star Struck One Nighter is a completely baseless accusation of rape. Often the One Nighter will encounter the athlete while under the influence of liquor or drugs and be unable to restrain herself. Often the athlete will be intoxicated, as well and unable to restrain himself. The two will partake in a totally consensual sexual encounter, but after the deed is done, the Star Struck One Nighter often wakes up not fully knowing what she has done, or intensely embarrassed about what she knows she has done. The girl does not want to be viewed around campus as "easy" and most girls don't want the title of Jersey Chaser/Star Struck One Nighter. So, the one way to protect her reputation and save face is for her to scream, "He forced me!" I have seen this with my own eyes. The toll it will take on the athlete's life is enormous.

I witnessed this story-line play out up close and personal while attending the University of Iowa. Abe Satterfeild, a defensive back that was recruited from Pennsylvania and good friend of mine, found himself in the position of the young black male athlete who had become entangled with a Star Struck One Nighter. That mistake would end up costing him almost everything. Late one weekend night myself and a few other players were hanging out at Hill Crest dormitory. As we hung out we witnessed Abe and a Caucasian female walking towards us, into the dorm and towards his room. Abe did not seem very anxious to go into the room with the girl, but she seemed to be coercing or leading him to a place she wanted to go. We all knew what the situation was, as it was not uncommon for Star Struck One Nighters to throw themselves at football players and refuse to take no for an answer. The two went into the room and did what hormone driven college kids often do, but that night changed both of their lives forever.

In the days following that encounter, the girl accused Abe of rape. Abe vehemently denied the allegation and made clear to all of us that the female had in fact been the aggressor and initiator of the sexual activity. All of us who observed the girl's body language as she led Abe into the room, had no doubt that Abe was telling the truth. None of that mattered to the police or the media. Abe was arrested and the media circus began. Abe's face was in the campus newspaper everyday non-stop as endless articles about the allegations were pumped out. The talk of the town was centered on this controversy, whether Abe was guilty or the girl was lying. Abe was facing up to 60 years in prison and his entire life was thrown into disarray. In the end the prosecutor agreed to allow Abe to plead guilty to a much less serious charge, a misdemeanor in fact. I presume this is because of the lack of evidence the state had against the young man. Abe maintained that he had not forced the girl throughout the ordeal and in the end he turned out to be telling the truth.

Exoneration, right? Things would return to normal and Abe would be allowed to return to his classes and his football team, right? Absolutely not! Abe's name had been tarnished and dragged through the mud so thoroughly that he could never return to his old life as a student athlete at the University of Iowa. His name was no longer Abe Satterfield, it was now The Accused Rapist Abe Satterfield. Wherever he went in the city, from class to the library to the corner store, there would be stares, whispers and funny looks. Those who supported Abe had long since forgiven him; others would never be able to do that. Abe spoke with the Iowa coaching staff, and both sides agreed that the best way forward for the young man was a clean break with Iowa. Abe would be forced to abandon his dream of being a Hawkeye defensive back. He would have to pack up his life and move across the country. He would have to start all over, with the cloud of that horrible accusation hanging over his head forever. All of this for a night of pleasure with a Star Struck One Nighter.

In addition to the hardship experienced by the wrongfully accused Abe Satterfield, the life of the young woman involved would never be the same again. Many people saw her as an innocent victim in the situation, but a large portion of the university community viewed her as a promiscuous opportunist who had ruined the life of an innocent young man in order to attempt to save face after one of her sexual escapades. She received threats from other students at the university, and her life would never be permitted to return to normal in Iowa City. She too ended up leaving the university, having to start all over elsewhere with this painful ordeal looming over her head.

I detail this chain of events not to target the young woman involved and I do not aim to shame her in any way. In addition, I understand perfectly that rape is a major problem on college campuses around the country and that every year many young women are forced into sexual acts against their will. I understand that male athletes in fact commit rapes against women who clearly manifest their unwillingness to engage in sex. It must be stated though that there are many cases when the women go along willingly and later for some reason or another simply are embarrassed that they did so. For this reason I tell this story to warn young black male athletes around the country. Sure, your next casual sexual encounter with a Star Struck One Nighter could turn out to be nothing more than a fun night of sexual pleasure. Or, it could turn out to be the absolute worst mistake you have ever made in your life; bringing permanent pain, shame and disgrace to you and your family. If you want to risk it, go ahead, but I'd bet if Abe Satterfeild had the chance to do it all again, he would give up that night of pleasure in a heart beat.

The Jersey Chaser and the Star Struck One Nighter are major traps that many young athletes fall into.

# TOO MUCH FREEDOM AND TOO MUCH FUN:

THE FREEDOM, AUTONOMY and fun that come with going away from home to attend college and play sports can create enduring memories that make college the best years of a man's life. Unfortunately, they can also give a man life long regrets. When many young black males arrive on the campus of a large institution, they are away from their parents and home environments for the first time. Their coaches provide supervision to a certain extent, but for the most part the young men must make their own decisions. They have a student body around them that looks up to them and wants to socialize with them. How they handle these circumstances can determine whether they seize the opportunity that they've earned, or throw it all away.

The mature route for these men is to socialize and celebrate in moderation, never allowing partying and drinking to interfere with their academic work or their athletic training and preparation. These young men must be careful not to let the weekend bleed into their workweek to the extent that the weekend never ends. Drinking will occur on college campuses, but drinking too much and too frequently are things these young men must avoid. I can speak from personal experience when saying that too much liquor will cause you to make costly mistakes that you never would have made while sober. If you limit the weekend to Friday and Saturday and avoid excessive drinking and drugs, the social aspect of college can be fun and rewarding. If you are unable to restrain and discipline yourself in the face of unlimited freedom, the results can be devastating and embarrassing.

While in college as a freshman, I had a roommate who was a stunning example of too much partying and too much freedom. As I stated above, from the moment this young man stepped on campus he was overly excited about the chance to go out, drink, meet women, sleep with women, and wake up and do it all over again. He had a tough time making it to morning workouts because he had very long nights. He often slept through class because he had very long nights. He could not keep his weight at the level desired by the strength and conditioning staff because he drank a lot on those very long nights. After one year his GPA was below the 2.0 mark, to the extent that he didn't even qualify to go on academic probation. He did not return for his second year, all because he was unable to limit the weekend to the actual weekend and drink and socialize in moderation.

Once I finished playing football and began to experience

an added level of freedom and autonomy, I also took drinking and partying too far. It never affected my academic performance, as I was a serious student. Unfortunately, it did however lead to fights downtown, trouble with the law, and life long regrets. I was arrested on multiple occasions and though every charge seemed minor (a public misconduct here, a public intoxication there) those stupid, petty incidents took on an extraordinary level of importance as I applied to law schools, and after I had finished law school and was applying to the Florida bar. I have volunteered and worked many jobs involving black inner city youth (which is my life's passion), and before I could participate in each of those endeavors I had to account for and try to explain every stupid run-in with the law that I had in Iowa City. Had I known while I was partying what the results would be, I would have slowed down big time, but who thinks about that stuff while they're taking shots of vodka and playing beer pong?

Thank God I was able to see the big picture before it was too late. After seeing my future flash before my eyes while sitting in a cell in the Iowa City jail, I realized that I had to grow up. I developed a strict set of rules that applied whenever I planned on going out. I would stay away from the infamous down town "Ped Mall" area where thousands of drunken kids congregate every Saturday in Iowa City. I would always go out with a friend that was more mature and cool-headed than I was to insure that if something happened cooler heads would prevail. I would never drink if I had to drive and I would stop drinking at any point that

I felt the effects too strongly. I still enjoyed going out and socializing after I instituted these rules, but I was able to do so without worrying about waking up in a cell the next morning. Maturity and moderation are essential to having fun, without throwing away everything that you've worked so hard to achieve.

Another trap that goes hand in hand with the too much freedom-too much fun trap, is what I call the "Friend With A Motive." On every college campus there are students and citizens in the community that will seek to befriend student athletes for the sole purpose of benefitting from the relationship in some way. These individuals do not particularly care about the student athlete, but do care about how they can benefit from being around or utilizing the student athlete. One example of this was a man I met in Iowa City who seemed just to want to help me out and ensure I had the things I needed while in school. "Cool guy" I thought, until I realized his true motive was to up the sells at the card shop that he owned. His biggest sellers were Iowa Hawkeye football player cards and he thought it would be nice if he could get me and possibly other Hawkeye football players to help pub his store or sign cards. The only problem is that the NCAA has very strict rules on this type of thing, and the compensation he was offering for our help could have landed us in a terrible situation.

Another example of a dangerous Friend With A Motive was a student I met during my 2nd year at Iowa. This young man was always anxious to have me come to parties or bars with him. The problem is that he was a complete hot head and would invariably end up in fights. He was a non-athlete though, so his name would never end up on the front page of the paper the next morning. He would always look to me to step in and help fight his battles, which was the absolute last thing I needed to do. I was good enough at getting into trouble on my own and definitely did not need to take on another guy's battles. As I matured though, it occurred to me that fighting his battles was exactly why this student always wanted me with him when he went out. I quickly ended that "friendship," and excised that person from my life. Whether it is some overly friendly individual seeking to up his business profits off of you, or another student who wants you to fight his battles or "hook him up with game tickets," you must be very careful about whom you allow to hang around you. You have a lot more to lose than they do and they can bring you down.

# FAILURE TO RECOGNIZE THE OPPORTUNITY AT HAND:

THE OPPORTUNITY TO receive an education at a respected institution of higher learning, to accumulate no debt while receiving this education, and to compete at the highest levels athletically, is rare and worth cherishing. Many student athletes cherish the athletic opportunity that is before them while not fully appreciating the academic opportunity. Some do not even fully recognize the value of the athletic opportunity they are faced with, and simply go through the athletic motions of practice and training each day. The tough yet rewarding thing for a young student athlete to do is to appreciate both aspects of the college experience and put maximum effort into both.

A student athlete should find a major that he is interested in and work toward getting the highest grades possible, not simply staying eligible to play. He should attend class and study as well as lifting weights and watching game film. He should get enough sleep so that he not only has energy at practice, but also has the energy to actively learn and participate in class. He should learn to respect the prowess and credentials of his professors as much as he respects the position and accomplishments of his coaches and the alumni from his school that went on to play professionally. I've seen athletes that were starters for multiple seasons at Iowa while also earning engineering degrees and graduating with honors. I've also seen starters at Iowa earn degrees in biology and go on to medical school. I've seen players get degrees in communications and go on to well paying careers in that field. There is no rule that athletes have to be jocks that do just enough academically to get by. The players that get the most out of college and set themselves up for the most success in the future are the ones who appreciate both the academic and athletic opportunities that they are faced with, and put maximum effort into both.

At the University of Iowa I did not limit myself to just getting by academically or to the athletic circle of friends, like many athletes do. I was as committed in the classroom as I was in the weight-room and so despite a career ending injury, I graduated in four years with honors in political science. I stepped outside of the normal "football player box" and got involved in serving the community, student government and national politics. By the time my four years at Iowa were up, I had served as a senator in the student government, met the future president of the United States on multiple occasions (as I worked with the Barack Obama Campaign) and helped launch an awesome after school mentoring program for disadvantaged kids in the area. Doing all of these things allowed me to broaden my horizons and learn a great deal. In addition, I met and formed lasting relationships with many excellent people. I began to understand the meaning of the saying "its not what you know, its who you know." Because of the great people that I met and worked with, whenever I needed anything, from a letter of recommendation for law school to a place to sleep when I'm back in town and even jobs while I was in Iowa City; I always had a connection that I could call on. It is not smart or beneficial for you to limit yourself to playing football, just surviving academically and living in the football bubble. There are lifelong benefits to taking your academics serious, broadening your horizons and getting involved in other things.

# CAMPUS ATHLETE HATERS:

YOUNG MEN HEADED to college must be aware that just as there were "haters" in high school, there will be students in college who hate all athletes, simply because they are athletes. These "haters" despise football and basketball players for a variety of different reasons. Some haters are simply jealous of athletes. They see athletes as spoiled, pampered and undeserving, yet they have no idea what a college athlete has to endure in order to be dominant on and off the field. These haters will go out of their way to disparage, embarrass and "one up" athletes on campus. They wait for an athlete's face to end up on the front page of the paper (for a negative reason) so that they can point to that as proof that all athletes are irresponsible and unintelligent. These haters despise the fact that the school offers athletes free education and provides housing, books, etc., for them. The haters do not understand the exposure and notoriety that athletes bring to universities, and only see what the athlete is getting from the university. These haters are very dangerous people, and athletes should simply avoid them as much as possible.

I had a rough experience during my college years with a "football player hater." At a fraternity party during my junior year, I got into a confrontation with some fraternity brothers. One of my female friends stepped between us to keep anything from happening. There was a little mild shoving but nothing serious broke out. Unfortunately for me, the minor confrontation attracted the attention of cops, as there were many on hand for the event. I was charged with a public intoxication (I had in fact been drinking) but the cops chose to also charge me with a battery because of the shoving. I felt that was totally unjustifiable and unnecessary considering my female friend informed the cops that no punches were exchanged and that it was a brief confrontation. At my trial though, a young man who was present at the event (though he was not involved in the conflict) showed up to testify against me, he was the only witness the state had. He got on the stand and told a wildly exaggerated tale about me shoving and hitting my own friend who had stepped in to de-escalate the situation. I could not believe his story and was totally flabbergasted by it. I had never seen the individual and did not understand why he would come to court and testify falsely against me. The judge found his testimony particularly convincing because he appeared to be a totally "disinterested" witness who just wanted the truth to come out. He was anything but that.

After the entire situation was resolved I found out who

the guy was and why he wanted to see me punished as harshly as possible. It turned out that a few months prior to my incident, the "disinterested witness" and his friends had gotten into a fight with a few football players. Apparently the football players had gotten the best of the guy and his friends leaving them pretty embarrassed. As a result, this guy grew to hate all Iowa football players even more than he did in the first place. By the time my incident occurred, I was no longer even playing football, but this guy still saw it as an opportunity to stick it to a football player. He drove in the morning of my trial from another city just to make sure he got some form of revenge on an Iowa football player.

This is the level of hatred and jealousy that some on campus harbor when it comes to athletes. When a young athlete gets to campus he must learn how to spot these haters and avoid them. Don't socialize with them. Don't hang out in the same places that they do, STAY AS FOR AWAY FROM THEM AS POSSIBLE. The young man who came to testify against me could have cost me a lot had it not been for a judge who cut me a break. These haters can hurt a young athlete in many serious ways.

# GREED IS THE ROOT OF ALL EVIL:

THE MOMENT A young athlete steps onto campus at a large university there will be countless ways for him to rake in numerous financial and other benefits simply because of his status as an athlete. Almost every one of those benefits can lead to serious trouble and the downfall of the athlete. The ways a college football player can utilize his status as an athlete to reap some sort of financial reward are endless, so I will list just a few that I know happen frequently.

1) Direct gifts from boosters including money, cars, clothes, etc.

2) Gifts and benefits from citizens in the local business community such as free meals, drinks, cars, tattoos, etc.

3) Scalpers that will pay big money for the game seats that all players get for free.

4) Local club owners allowing athletes free entry, free drinks, etc, because they know the presence of athletes in their establishments will attract other patrons.

5) Schemers who will get athletes to autograph memorabilia so that they can sell it while promising the athlete a kick back.

6) Schools using indirect methods to essentially pay student athletes.

This list could go on for days. This trap is especially dangerous for athletes like myself who come from impoverished circumstances. We do not have parents that can simply send us a few hundred dollars whenever we get low on funds. Athletic scholarships cover a lot, but they do not cover everything. If a kid needs to fly home for an emergency or just wants to visit his family, he has to come up with that money on his own. If the kid wants to buy a laptop for class or needs a new jacket, he's on his own. If he simply wants to take a girl out for dinner, he has to come up with the money on his own. For this reason, using your status as an athlete to make a quick profit becomes a very appealing idea to many young men. The sad part is that some young men who do not even come from impoverished families, seem to show up on campus with the decision already made that they will use their status as athletes to rake in as much money and gifts as possible, as quickly as possible. These things almost always go wrong; the Cam Newton "Pay to Play" scandal, the Terrelle Pryor free tattoo scandal at Ohio State, and the Reggie Bush "Heisman trophy take back scandal", are just a few examples of this. I saw this type of thing up close and personal at Iowa with a standout wide receiver by the name of Dominque Douglass. This kid was from inner city Detroit and had a set of the surest hands I had ever seen. His ability to step on the field as a true freshman and make clutch catches left us all dumbfounded. His inability to keep his hands off of stuff that was not his left his career and life in shambles. He was arrested multiple times for theft type offenses, and eventually kicked off of the team.

What I want you to take away from this rule is twofold: 1) For the players that actually need financial help to get by, be very careful what gifts and benefits of any sort that you accept from anyone. Even if you did not intend to break any NCAA rules, it can come back to haunt you. 2) For the players that simply want to "cash in" on their status as star athletes, think about whether it is worth the risk of jail and or getting kicked off of the team. The simple benefits you gain here and there can cost you everything in the end.

These are the main traps that I've discovered from my experience as a student athlete, a student, and in that peculiar position between the two, along with study and thought after leaving Iowa City. I sincerely hope and pray that the warnings provided within this book will reach inner city black males as they navigate life on and off of the gridiron. It is my greatest hope that parents will give this book to their sons while they are in high school or as they go off to college so that they will have the foresight to avoid these traps. My heart truly breaks each and every time I speak with an inner city black male who earned an athletic scholarship and the chance to improve his entire life, but because he fell into one of these traps he is back in the ghetto telling stories of his glory days, with ABSOLUTELY NOTHING TO SHOW FOR IT.

# MY OWN JOURNEY:

I WAS BORN AND raised in Orlando, Florida, one of six children. I lived my entire life in the tougher, higher crime, impoverished areas of the city. My mom bore the burden of raising us with almost no help from my dad who battled drug and alcohol problems in addition to a violent temper. My mom worked extremely hard every day of her life, but ends still did not always meet. Despite the fact that there was not a single day where my mom was not working at least one job, there were times when we found ourselves without lights, running water, and various other essential components of a decent standard of living.

Throughout that time there were two constants in my life, God and football. My mom has always been a strong Christian and she instilled these principles in her children. She made sure we were all in church every Sunday. Aside from God, football was my life. It was my hobby, it was my social life and most importantly, it provided the only route I could see at that time to lift my family out of poverty. I began training for football around the age of 7 or 8. I would run, lift and compete everyday attempting to build myself into an unstoppable football player. I watched football on TV, I read about football in the newspaper and in magazines, the only video games I played were Madden NFL football and NCAA football. Football was my life.

In high school I put some added effort into my academics because I knew that in order to get to college and play football, I had to qualify academically. The school I attended was a struggling school that had been given the grade F for multiple years under the "No Child Left Behind" grading system. Despite that, I remained focused on becoming the very best football player in the country and getting grades that were good enough to go to college. I started 3 years on the varsity team, I was second team All-State as a senior, I was a champion in high school power lifting and an undefeated conference and regional heavy weight champion in wrestling. I did all those things for the purpose of getting a Division One football scholarship and as a senior I was blessed with that opportunity. I received a full scholarship to attend the University of Iowa and I was thrilled to be headed to compete in the Big Ten.

Receiving a scholarship to the University of Iowa was one of the proudest moments of my life. I was a defensive tackle and the University of Iowa had earned a reputation for producing strong, tough defensive linemen that went on to do very well in the NFL. Jonathan Babinaux, Matt Roth and Colin Cole were just a few of the more recent Iowa defensive linemen that were then playing professionally. My life long goal had been to make it to the NFL and getting a scholarship to a school like Iowa would greatly increase the likelihood of me reaching that goal. I was ready to pursue my dream and do whatever was needed to make it come true.

Upon my arrival in Iowa City, I dove head first into training and preparing for the upcoming season. I arrived in Iowa City early so that I could participate in the team's summer conditioning program. It was grueling and eye opening, but I felt like I was doing what needed to be done for me to reach my goal. As a Florida kid, I was a bit surprised to find out that Iowa City boasted 95-degree temperatures throughout the summer and so I would in no way be escaping the heat. I knew that Iowa head strength and conditioning coach, Chris Doyle, had a reputation as one of the most intense and effective strength coaches in the country, and he did not disappoint me. The summer program was intense, comprehensive and dead serious involving everything from pulling sleds, pushing farm carts, heavy lifting and endless running. Summer lifting was tough, but it was nothing compared to training camp two-a-days. That short but intense span caused me, and I'm sure every other player, to question whether football was really what we wanted to do with our lives.

I was redshirted as a true freshman. I spent that season training hard in the weight room and working hard in the classroom. My main responsibility to the team on the practice field was to prepare the starters for each game by competing on the scout team. That season allowed me to grow and learn a lot about the game. I put in extra work to improve my foot speed (my main area of concern) and it paid off. By the time spring football rolled around leading into my redshirt freshman year, I was a completely different player. Where as upon my arrival everything seemed to move too fast for me on the field, by the spring things had slowed down. My agility had improved and the fact that I was one of the strongest players on the team created a formidable combination. I was making big plays each day of practice and opening eyes. I moved up the depth chart and though we had returning starters (Matt Krouhl and Mitch King) it was clear that I would receive major playing time. I went from questioning my future in football to loving the game again. My dreams seemed closer than ever before, as I would be playing substantial reps for the Iowa Hawkeyes in the Big Ten conference as a redshirt freshman. I was riding high, until "disaster" happened.

During one of the final practices as we neared the end of spring football, another defensive lineman was driven into the side of my knee. The weight of the player bent my knee inward into an unnatural position, which caused those who saw the collision to fear the worst. The collision did not result in an ACL tear, but it did further damage to my meniscus (which had been injured before) and broke off bone spurs within my knee joint. Further MRIs revealed that there was almost no meniscus left within the knee and that the overall cartilage was so worn out that there was no cushion between my tibia and my fibula. Where the two bones met in my leg was essentially bone on bone and arthritis had already set in. In addition, the structure of my other knee and past problems that I'd had with it made it likely that it could develop the same problems. I was faced with the most difficult decision of my life, whether to walk away from the game that I had built my life around or to risk my health in a serious way and push on with my dream.

In reality I made my decision fairly quickly after about three days of intense praying, thinking and debating within myself. I was not going to risk not being able to walk in the future in order to continue to play football. I reached the conclusion that there were other avenues that I could go down in life, which did not involve me sacrificing my joints, bones and ligaments. I still loved football, and I still loved Iowa football, but I loved my health more. I decided to focus on my academic performance and pursue other interests. Kirk Ferentz assured me that despite my injury, my education would still be fully paid for and I'd continue to receive every benefit I had as a player. I was and am extremely grateful for the open honest treatment that I continued to receive from Coach Ferentz, Chris Doyle, and the entire Iowa coaching staff. I decided to continue to lift with the team and help out coaching the defensive line. To that extent I remained engrained in the football culture. At that point I suddenly had a lot more time on my hands and this led to three important changes in my life. (1) I was able to put more time into my academics, which resulted in me graduating in four years with honors in political science. (2) I had more time and freedom to party and socialize which I took too far at times and suffered the consequences. (3) I was in a place just between being a student and a student athlete and my time in that peculiar position allowed me to make the observations that I based this list of rules upon.

I graduated from the University of Iowa in 2009 and enrolled at Florida Coastal School of Law in Jacksonville, Florida. There I was an honor student and received my Juris Doctorate in 2012. While at Florida Coastal, I wrote three in depth legal essays; all of which focused on the condition of impoverished black males in this country and the changes that must be made at the structural/legal level as well as at the personal level in order to change the condition of this group.

# NOTABLE ATHLETES
# WHO FELL INTO THESE TRAPS:

## WILLIE WILLIAMS
### Miami Carol City Linebacker: Signed to the University of Miami

Willie Williams is at the top of this list because his life
fully illustrates the story of a young urban black male
whose supreme athletic ability gave him endless opportunities, yet the traps above left him with nothing to show
for his efforts. More than anything, Willie's life may illus-
trate the trap of having no identity or aim in life aside from
that of being an athlete. This young man's troubles started
well before he entered college, but as long as Willie could
still find a way onto the football field he seemed content
in continuing in his irresponsible ways. After signing with
The University of Miami right out of high school, Williams
transferred to Louisville, after struggling at the U for two
seasons. While at Louisville Mr. Williams had more run-
ins with the law, which led to him being dismissed from

that team. Williams then transferred to a much smaller school and continued to dominate on the field, while not learning at all from his mistakes off the field.

There seems to have been no desire or motivation on his part to prepare himself for life beyond football or even any recognition of the fact that there was something called life without football. Willie Williams was the most highly recruited linebacker in the nation his senior year and every big football school in Florida rolled out the red carpet for this young man to come visit their campuses. His off the field issues caused him to bounce around to 5 different colleges throughout his career and yet not a single coach has ever doubted the high level of talent this kid possessed. He was as certain as certain can be to become a first round NFL draft pick, yet at the time that I'm writing this book he has never been on any NFL team and is facing criminal charges once again. Williams possessed excellent size, abnormal speed and rare God-given football instinct, but currently has NOTHING TO SHOW FOR IT.

## MAURICE CLARETT:
### Ohio State Running Back

Maurice Clarett took the nation by storm when he led the Ohio State Buckeyes to a national title as a true freshman in 2002. He was a 230-pound punishing runner with the speed to take any carry all the way. He was known as a dedicated worker on the practice field and viewed as a lock to carry on the long tradition of great Ohio State running backs to go on and dominate in the NFL.

The NFL greatness part never came true. Clarett attempted to enter the NFL after just one season of college football (and a subsequent school suspension for receiving improper gifts) but NFL rules prevented him from doing so. In 2005, the Denver Broncos gave Clarett his only chance to make it in the league, but his off the field life of partying, drinking and drugs led to him being cut after only a short time with that team. Shortly thereafter, Clarett was arrested for robbery and then re-arrested when he was caught with a bulletproof vest, assault rifle and hand guns ALLEGEDLY on his way to the home of the robbery victim to make sure the victim did not show up to testify at trial. That incident sent Clarett away for a lengthy prison sentence and probably put a permanent end to his dreams of ever getting back into the NFL.

If you look at the way Clarett lived while on campus for just one year, it becomes clear how he fell so far so fast. Clarett seems to have consistently and intentionally become caught in almost every single trap that I speak of above. He did not care the least about his education and getting a degree. He has spoken on several occasions about how he took golf and softball classes. He has also spoken about how he partied frequently and used a plethora of drugs. He had way too much freedom and way too much fun. He saw college as simply prep for the pros as he began living an NFL lifestyle way before he was even eligible to enter the NFL. Clarett also revealed that he was receiving large amounts of money, and owned three expensive cars while on campus.

Jersey Chasers were one of his favorite hobbies as he spent lots of time chasing women. And as with Willie Williams it seems that Clarett had no other identity or purpose in life aside from being a football player. In just a short time he went from the dream of national fame to the nightmare of a prison cell. Supreme talent, a national title, and now NOTHING TO SHOW FOR IT.

## CARLTON CHRISTIAN:
### Orlando High School Basketball Star: Signed with Marquette University

Carlton Christian is on this list mainly because I knew him personally and I watched the "I Wanna Go Home Syndrome" derail his career, first hand. Carlton and I grew up on the same street, Mercy Drive in Orlando, Florida. The street is known for its drugs, crime and violence. Carlton and I attended the same high school, Maynard Evans High, which is located in the middle of an area called Pine Hills (later nicknamed "Crime Hills"). Everyone in that area knows how hard it is for a kid to make it out, but Carlton beat all the odds. At 6'5 with the leaping ability of a high jumper Carlton jumped over all the hurdles that come with growing up in the ghetto. I watched him grow from a skinny kid into an athlete who was highly recruited by colleges all around the nation.

Carlton signed to Marquette and took the hopes of our community with him to Wisconsin. He played as a true freshman in 22 games contributing to the team in many different ways. We thought he was on track to become the standout player we knew him to be, but something put that to an end. After just one year away, something caused Carlton to desire to come back home. A strange tug on your heart and mind (which I experienced a bit while in Iowa) causes many of us who come from the ghetto to think it's safer and easier back closer to home. So Carlton came home and his fall from grace began immediately. He never played any significant role for the school that he transferred to, the University of Central Florida, and he has accumulated a lengthy criminal record since returning. He was nearly killed in an incident where he got into a gun fight which ended with his car being shot multiple times. The days of his domination on the hardwood seem so long ago and Carlton Christian has NOTHING TO SHOW FOR IT.

## SHONN GREENE:
### University of Iowa Running Back: New York Jets/ Tennessee Titans Running Back

Greene makes this list because his story, despite the fact that he ended up where he wanted to be, shows just how harmful a careless attitude regarding academics can be to a player's athletic dreams. Shonn Greene is one of the most impressive athletes I've ever seen. I've watched him lift and run, up close and he possesses a rare combination of size, speed and explosiveness. Before he was our star running back at Iowa, he would sprint down the field and destroy other players on our kick-off team. He was a fearless force on the football field. That intensity though did not carry over to the classroom.

After his sophomore season, Greene was forced to leave the University of Iowa because his grades were way too low. This promising NFL prospect was sent to a small community college in Iowa to try and bring his grades up to a level that would allow him to return to the University. No longer on the full scholarship that pays room, board, tuition and books Greene had to work for $8 an hour at a furniture factory. The days of performing in front of 70,000 adoring fans seemed to be just a thing of the past. I knew Shonn Greene personally at the University of Iowa and he is far from what some would call an unintelligent person. I knew he was capable the entire time of earning the grades that were required to compete, but he did not take class seriously. Academics, for many athletes like Greene, seem to be just a hassle or some annoying requirement as oppose to an area that should be stimulating and worthwhile. That approach to academics as some pesky unnecessary burden almost cost Greene everything.

Greene eventually realized that he had to put as much effort into his academics as he put into football. He got his grades up and came back to the University of Iowa in stunning fashion. He became an All-American, a Doak Walker Award winner and 3rd round draft pick by the New York Jets. Shonn Greene, unlike the other athletes on this list, has a lot to show for his efforts, but a lax academic approach almost put him into the same boat as Maurice Clarett.

## DOMINIQUE DOUGLASS:
### Former Standout Iowa Receiver

Dominique Douglass was a stand out prep athlete from inner city Detroit and was recruited to play wide receiver at Iowa during my time at the University. From the moment this young man stepped onto the football field we were all amazed at his extraordinary hands and ability to make big catches in clutch situations. It was unheard of for a true freshman to step right into Big Ten competition and catch the ball time after time in situations where the pressure was so high. We all thought the sky was the limit for the young man. We were wrong.

In addition to Douglass being able to get his hands on the ball, he had a relentless desire to get his hands on money and other material things that did not belong to him. He is the most concrete example that I've met personally of a college football player who sought to utilize his status to rake in as many financial and other benefits as possible, as quickly as possible. His endless pursuit of these benefits led to him being arrested for credit card fraud in August of 2007. He had made unauthorized use of someone else's credit card. The boat didn't stop there as just two months later, he was caught stealing out of a Wal-Mart. Then things really got bad. After being suspended indefinitely from the team and returning to Detroit, Douglass was arrested for an armed robbery. The story of a young man who climbed very high very fast only to fall even faster played itself out again.

I do not think it was actual need that drove Douglass to try to cash in on his status as a football player at every turn. It seems to be simple greed and materialism that drove him to do many of the things he did. His desire to cash in left him with nothing to show for a record setting freshman year at the University of Iowa.

In conclusion, I urge every young athlete who reads this book to take full advantage of the opportunities that you have worked so hard to earn. Do not fall into the traps that I list above and end up with Nothing To Show for all of your hard work.

# AUTHOR'S NOTE:

As this book was being edited in the fall of 2013 a gripping story shook the entire world of college football to the core. This "scandal" served as further proof of the assertions and prescriptions laid out in this book. The dynamics discussed in Trap Number 5, "Jersey Chasers and Star Struck One-nighters", were played out yet again for the whole nation to see as then Heisman trophy candidate and quarterback for the number one ranked, undefeated Florida State Seminoles, Jameis Winston became the focus of a sexual battery investigation.

Jameis Winston grew up a two-sport standout athlete in Hueytown, Alabama. He spoke about the trying circumstances that he and his family faced at times throughout his life. There were stints when Winston's dad was without a job and the family had to rely on young Winston to bring home money to buy food and pay bills. Winston was focused and determined enough to prevail over these circumstances and earn a scholarship to Florida State University (FSU).

From the moment Winston walked on campus he wowed his teammates and coaches with his extraordinary ability and uncanny charisma. He seemed to be a born leader and became the team's starting QB as a true freshman. That was just the start.

Jameis Winston took Florida State through a dream season, setting multiple passing records and not losing a single game. As the fall of 2013 came to a close, it was clear that undefeated FSU would be playing for a national title and their superstar freshman QB was a shoe in for the Heisman trophy. This magical run was thrown into jeopardy when an allegation of a rape surfaced. A female student from FSU claimed that Winston sexually assaulted her nearly a year prior to the accusations. The nation held its breath waiting to see if charges would be filed against Winston.

As facts surrounding the case began to leak out, it became evident to me that this entire debacle was a classic example of falling into trap number 5: Jersey Chasers and Star Struck One-nighters. The accuser was an "acquaintance" of Winston's, as there were multiple photos of the two together on previous occasions; this fact made the accuser's allegation more bizarre as she initially claimed to not have known her attacker. Rumors circulated on the internet that Winston and the accuser had "hooked up" on multiple occasions in the past and the only thing different about the encounter on the night in question was that the accuser became very angry when Winston let her know that he couldn't stay with her because his girlfriend was going to be in town soon.

Winston maintained throughout the ordeal that the two had had consensual sex. The investigation revealed that on the night in question, Winston's DNA had been found in the victim's panties, along with the DNA of another male. It also became known that the accuser and a group of her friends identified themselves as "cleat chasers" and frequently used that phrase as a hash tag on Twitter. Eventually prosecutors decided that there was insufficient evidence to proceed with filing charges. Winston would not be charged, arrested, tried or convicted.

One must consider all the things that hung in absolute peril because Winston fell into trap number 5. As a 6'4, 235 pound QB with excellent mobility and great arm strength, Winston certainly fits the mold of a first round NFL QB. When these allegations came to light, Winston was leading his team to victory after victory and putting up numbers that eventually won him the coveted Heisman trophy. Clearly on a path toward greatness, Winston suddenly faced the real possibility of serving life in prison (depending on the particulars of the charges). Had charges been filed there would have been no Heisman trophy, no national championship game and no first round NFL signing bonus. The name of this freshman phenom would have been uttered in the same category as Maurice Clarett. Jameis Winston would have had plenty of time to contemplate whether or not he could have done without the thrill of a Jersey Chaser.

Made in the USA
San Bernardino, CA
23 May 2019